INQUIRE WITHIN

INQUIRE WITHIN

Poems by

IN-Q

Illustrations by Mustashrik Mahbub

HarperOne
An Imprint of HarperCollins*Publishers*

HarperOne

HarperCollins books may be purchased for educational, business, or sales promotional use. For information, please email the Special Markets Department at SPsales@harpercollins.com.

Illustrations by Mustashrik Mahbub

FIRST EDITION

Library of Congress Cataloging-in-Publication Data

Names: Schmalholz, Adam, author.
Title: Inquire within / Adam Schmalholz.
Description: San Francisco : HarperOne, 2020.
Identifiers: LCCN 2019030896 (print) | LCCN 2019030897 (ebook) |
    ISBN 9780062954701 (hardcover) | ISBN 9780062954725 | ISBN 9780062954749 |
    ISBN 9780062954718 (ebook)
Subjects: LCSH: Awareness—Poetry. | Conduct of life—Poetry. | Self-realization—Poetry.
    LCGFT: Poetry.
Classification: LCC PS3619.C4423 I57 2020 (print) | LCC PS3619.C4423 (ebook) |
    DDC 811/.6—dc23
LC record available at https://lccn.loc.gov/2019030896
LC ebook record available at https://lccn.loc.gov/2019030897

20 21 22 23 24   LSC   10 9 8 7 6 5 4 3 2 1

Defining myself

Is like confining myself

So I undefined myself

To find myself

PART ONE
INHALE

All Your Light

I keep my heart open, but I rarely give it away
People don't know what to do
With other people's hearts these days
They use them and abuse them in the most codependent ways
That's why for many years, I locked my heart behind my rib cage

But that hurt me more than all the pain that I was being saved
Because if you don't use your heart
You might as well go dig your grave
And once you've turned it off
It's hard to find the switch to turn it on again
It never fully heals, it just covers up the holes within
And it will stay that way until you choose to go within
Or meet someone else, who triggers you into your suffering

Real heartbreak is a tool that helps reveal
The pain you couldn't feel
So it can truly heal

And as the layers peel
You get to deal with all the lies you hid behind
And all the times you tricked your mind
Convincing people *it was fine, you were fine, they were fine*
Everything was really fine
And you believed it over time
Closing all the blinds so you didn't have to see the shine

You showed up just enough to never really risk a thing
Making up excuses for keeping us at arm's length
Now you're risking everything
How's it feel to be alive?
Witness all the love and hate that you have hidden deep inside

If you can meet me halfway
I can take the whole truth

You're like the sun's rays peeking through a straw roof
I can sense how much you wanna show me all your light
And yet it's scary 'cause you'll also show your darkest night

Of course I'm scared too
I'm not invincible
But I would rather be seen than be invisible

Father Time

I'm staring at the number, wondering if I should call
I can hear the *tick tock* from the clock on the wall
As it meshes with the *thump thump* beat of my heart
Sometimes getting something started is the hardest part

I didn't meet my dad until I was fifteen

I had seen his photograph, but his image was sickening
A coward with a dick, but no balls to back it up
See, when he left me as a kid, I had cause for acting up

The funny thing about hate
Is the person you hate
Doesn't feel that hate
You feel that hate
But wait

The weight can be too much for a person to take
And personally I was hurt, so I locked it away

I was angry all the time and I didn't know why
I couldn't handle my rage so I would hide it inside
Pretending everything's fine became a daily pastime
Time passed and I started to believe in my own lies
I took it out on my mom because she raised me alone
The rage I couldn't own had left me totally numb
It was like land mines in my mind that I didn't understand
So when the boy inside cried, the young man outside yelled

I think I learned about my masculinity from TV
The people weren't real, so I knew they couldn't leave me

I'd sit there for hours right in front of the tube
The images that I saw were my depiction of truth
It was manhood in a box, and I bought into it
The censorship of anything inside of me that's sensitive
The sentence is a lifetime of tears suppressed in a stone face
An overblown ego they've distracted through a paper chase

Back when I was nine, I imagined in my mind
That my father was a spy working for the FBI
And that's why he couldn't stop by, write, or drop a line
He was off saving our lives from the bad guys
But that was just a lie that I used to get by
So that you wouldn't see the tears welling up in my eyes

When you're rejected by the person that you're created by
You secretly feel like you don't have a right to your life

I thought if I confronted him then it would make it alright
But since I couldn't forgive him, it just recycled my spite

I remember meeting him for the first time
Every time a person passed by I would ask
Mom, is that him?
I look a little like him, right?
No? Oh.
Well, what about that guy?
And that was what it was like
To meet the man that gave me my life
To shake his hand and look into his eyes
We talked till he apologized, then said our goodbyes
I walked away on my own then I began to cry

Now, for years after that I acted like it was all resolved
I'd told him what I thought, so I figured problem solved
But it just re-evolved
My insecurities were eating at my mental health
I took it out on the world because I hated myself
That's when I finally decided I needed some help

I opened up and started writing about my past
I got honest with myself and started chipping at my mask
I looked into the mirror and confronted what I saw
Accepting the reflection by embracing every flaw
Then directing the connection into breaking down the walls
By reflecting the perfection of the God inside us all

I stopped focusing on everything that I'd been hateful for
And started focusing on everything that I'm grateful for

And personally there is a lot I can be thankful for
If pain is dragging you down, just cut the ankle cord

That's when the weight lifted and I really started living
That's when my hate shifted and I really started giving
That's when my fate twisted, it was like an ego exorcism
Your mind state can be the most powerful of prisons

My father never played catch with me, or gave advice
But if nothing else, that man gave me my life
And that's enough for me, if that's all he can ever give
'Cause I'm appreciative for every day I get to live
And even though I don't need my dad to validate me
I thought that I should write this poem
To thank him for creating me

Because every moment we are alive is like a gift
And if that's not enough to forgive, then what is?

I'm staring at the number, wondering if I should call
I can hear the *tick tock* from the clock on the wall
As it meshes with the *thump thump* beat of my heart
Sometimes getting something started is the hardest part

I pick the phone up, the dial tone begins to *sing*
I punch his number into it, and it begins to . . .

Ring

Ring

Ring

Hello?

Hey Mike

It's Adam . . .

Your son

For Mom

There's an eight-year-old frozen in your heart
I see her every time you smile
She crawls out of her hiding place and dances for a while
She's careless and she's wild, not a worry in the world
The way we all should be as little boys and little girls
Something must have happened to her
But I can't say what it is
Her secret isn't mine to tell
It isn't mine to live
Her childhood was stolen
So her grown-up is a kid
Her heart is overwhelming
So she shows up in her head
I tried to make it better but I know I never did
Despite my best attempts
My intentions turned to shit

I cannot feel your pain for you
That only makes it worse

I cannot heal for you
But I can love the part of you that hurts

What if it was your mother? Your sister? Your lover?
What if it was your father? Your uncle? Your brother?
Ask yourself, what would you do?
If you knew? If you saw?
Would you speak? Or be weak?
Would you stand? Would you fall?
Even if we're not the problem
It's a problem for us all
Would you write? Would you call?
If you knew? If you saw?

All the people frozen in her heart are starting to unthaw
There is one for every age she was convinced it was her fault
If I could only unscrew my grandfather's locked jaw
She wouldn't need to keep her shame in an impenetrable vault
It's like looking at a diamond when you're focused on the flaw
Being this close, you don't see yourself the way you are from afar
The sun doesn't know that it's a star
It just feels the heat and it burns till it's gone

I ask if something's wrong
She's calm but won't respond

The tears begin to come

Who cares where they are from

It's better out than in, and she's held it in so long

The tears begin to come

Who cares where they are from

They fall with such perfection that the witness is undone

They ripple her reflection and she sees what she's become

There is one for every year and every fear she's overcome

She has never been a victim

And the alchemy is done

I didn't understand a man's privilege being young

It's hard to fight a war when you're unaware you've won

My father would have killed me but she chose to be a mom

She chose to be my mom

I chose her as my mom

He disowned me in his will even after he was gone

He wouldn't hold me as a baby or accept I was his son

My father didn't love me but you chose to be a mom

You chose to be my mom

I chose you as my mom

It shows in all you've done, and everything you still do

There must have been an eight-year-old frozen in my heart too

I'm sorry that I couldn't see it beyond the pain I'd been through
I'm sorry that I couldn't see it beyond my own point of view
I'm sorry that I couldn't see it
But I'm grateful I do

You will always be my mom
But it's nice to see you

Growing Up

Growing up is about learning
            then unlearning
                        everything we've learned
It's about constructing
            then deconstructing
                      who we are at every turn
Disrupting
            being
                      in
            the
flow

to contemplate
the tide

Then letting go again
                  to take the ride
                            without your mind

Home

I wanna buy a house where I can make memories in every room
Plant a garden in my backyard, and watch the flowers bloom
It will be big
But not so big that guests would get lost
It will be nice
But not so nice that everybody whispers, "What'd it cost?"
It will have gorgeous views
But being higher doesn't mean superior
I've learned not to judge a house by what's on the exterior
It's what's on the interior, and I don't mean design
Because a house is not a home unless the people are aligned

I used to want a mansion, I thought that'd bring me joy
I went and bought a lotta stuff that I had no time to enjoy
I was working for a living
But it wasn't working 'cause I wasn't living
And a life without living is unfulfilling
Filling up the empty space with all the things I was getting

Yet I could never get enough, or give enough, to be enough
And that was constantly upsetting

Value is a tricky thing
Is it something that we own?
Or is it something that we bring?

Experience is priceless and it doesn't cost a thing
'Cause once you make your mind up
You can accomplish anything
Even if it seems impossible
Impossible is possible
We take for granted that defying gravity is illogical
Intend what you desire and your will *will* be unstoppable

See, hope can be despair in disguise
So instead I decide, then I watch as reality realigns

Besides, what is time if it's different in a different place?
We're all in one place, floating out in outer space
They'll never bottle time
We can't buy any more
And if we could it'd be sold out at every corner store
So lately I've been thinking, what if less is really more?
If my mortality is what I'm really living for?

I wanna slide in socks across Italian marble floors
I want imported art to fill up every corridor
I want my kids to use my bed like it's their trampoline
To walk on top of my couch like it's their balance beam
I wanna use my things, so they aren't using me
After all, the most important things in life are free

We only borrow land
We only borrow time
We only borrow love
But you can borrow mine
My house is your house
Stay over anytime
If you're a friend you'll have a permanent vacancy sign

Community is what our culture's lacking
We pretend to be connected, but mostly it's just unscripted acting

We isolate ourselves and hide from our emotions
Then pack our schedules as an excuse to stay in motion
I'm living by the beach and yet I never see the ocean
It's always out of reach in the midst of my commotion
God forbid I'd have to sit alone without distraction
It's tough to notice thoughts when we're constantly in action
No matter what your status is, that isn't satisfaction

So I don't only care what you do
I care that you're doing it with *passion*

That's why we all should share our gifts and cultivate compassion
Because the fastest way to bliss
Is through a meaningful interaction
And since I'm not even sure that we exist, I've started asking
If this world of form is merely the illusion of attachment

If I could let it all go
My roof would be the stars
My floor would be the earth
My doors would be ajar
My walls would be the wind
My seat would be a stone
My bed would be the clouds
And my heart would be my home

But since I want a family and I don't live this life alone

I'm gonna buy a house
Where I can make memories in every room

Therapy

I was coming out of my new therapist's office the other day and sitting in the waiting room was my old therapist. It was awkward. I hadn't seen him since our final session, six years prior, and both of us were understandably caught off guard. There was an uncomfortable silence, followed by pleasantries.

"Hey, how are you?"

"Great," I said. "How are you?"

"Really good."

Another silence.

"Well, alright man. Take care of yourself," I said.

And I meant it.

He smiled. "You too, Adam."

I walked away shaking my head.

We are all going through this human shit together.

Say Yes

It's hard for me to say *yes*
It's easier for me to say *next year*
When the weather's fine
When I have the money, or the time
Or the relationship I want
Or the career, or the house, or the car, or the watch
Watch life pass me by waiting for an invitation
When the world is bigger than my nation
Or my occupation
The only thing I know
Is that we're all in this together
And the future of this earth
Depends on how we treat each other
But how we treat each other
Starts with how we treat ourselves
And how we treat ourselves
Starts with how we see ourselves

And how we see ourselves starts with context

Nothing can exist without its opposite

Remember this, the next time you find you're in an argument

And both sides are talking shit

And you forget your point

Except you're angry now and wanna win

So you continue yelling, till they give it up, by giving in

So you can stand victorious because you're right

On what again?

Do we laugh on instinct or do we choose to laugh?

Do we ask because we care or do we merely ask?

I ask you this because I care about how humans act

We're animals aware of our future and our past

And this can be an obstacle to traveling our path

Instead of just accepting where we're at

We analyze our tracks, for what we could have had

Looking back

Focused on the memories instead of on the facts

Hence what we attract

Still it's strange to factor in how fast it really flashes past

It's an exponential graph, from creation into ash

I'm sentimental one minute, then I'm making plans

Staking claims, shaking hands, breaking out or breaking in

I have about a billion mimes hidden underneath my skin

And they pull my face into this grin

Or push my wrinkled forehead in

So pour the gin, philosophize

No one has *your* awesome eyes

Your view is worth the lows and highs

You'll go through on this roller-coaster ride

Control has got us holding on

When letting go could be more fun

Hands up

Embrace the drop!

Eventually the fall will stop

Level out then come back up, until you reach another top

'Cause one day all your wheels fall off

So take advantage of your shocks

Do something you've never done

Do someone you've never done

Go someplace you've never gone

Someplace that will scare you some

Be someone you've never been

Feel all that adrenaline?

It's medicine to jump-start a spark inside your skeleton

See, everywhere you are is where you're supposed to be

So hopefully, you're hopelessly as lost as me

Because if you're not, you oughta be

Higher View

Life is all about you, and not at all about you
Now that's two opposing thoughts and yet both of them are true

How can we experience everything we choose to do
While observing the experience we're having from a higher view?

See, it's the question, not the answer that's the higher you
Otherwise you couldn't differentiate between the two

Awareness, but of who?

I am
the
journey
that I'm
getting to

Gratitude is my destination
My destiny is perfectly aligned with this location

I am the map, so my rhymes are like road signs
I have everything I want, 'cause my imagination's mine
But mine is not enough for me, 'cause I am not my mind
I could see it all and never get to see I'm truly blind
I could be it all but all identity is intertwined
The moon is only bright when it reflects the sun's shine
And I'm not entirely convinced I even write these lines
'Cause my DNA is coded by divine design

But if I manifest abundance while humanity is dying
I am equally responsible for all that I'm denying

See, you can tell the truth and still be lying
I did it for years
My perception was a fun-house mirror
And my projection was exaggerated on reality
Till my reflection back was nothing more than technicality

So who am I, if I'm not who I am?
What if I didn't have my name, or my age, or my friends?
If I didn't do my poetry, who would I be then?
The things that I've become are not the things I truly am

And everything I think I own, owns me in the end
Existence doesn't owe me anything

Quite the opposite
Existence will exist long after I am missed

So the art is more important than the artist is

Special Occasions

I used to save my clothes for special occasions that never came

There in the closet they would hang
Lonely, in the dark, waiting for me to change
But I was comfortable wearing my same things
My same shirts and my same jeans
My newer stuff was for the right time or right scene
I wouldn't waste them on a normal day of living

They were more for an event, or a premiere
Or the house party of the year
Where everyone was there, so they'd see me in my new gear
Rocking just the right look, so I could meet the right girl
And get her back to my house to get her clothes on my floor
But the tags were still on the collars
A couple seasons went by, my shit was out of style

So now I'm back in the aisle buying more stuff
I take it back to my closet and hang it all up

I wonder what they do when I'm not around

What if they come alive, climb down

Make believe they're me and run around?

Acting like they own the town

Mixing outfits and floating like ghosts off of the ground

I mean they probably wanna be used

If they could choose

Your shoes would try to break out of the box too

Kiss the concrete and learn to walk too

After all, that's what shoes were made to do

And even shoes wanna feel purposeful

What if chairs want to hold up our weight?

What if tables like when we gather around them to celebrate?

What if beds want to carry our dreams?

And we're taking them for granted

Because they're not living things

Then again, I've taken many living things for granted too

I could pass you on the street and barely notice you

'Cause if I noticed you, I'd see how beautiful you truly are

And yet the closer that we get

The more I feel our distance from afar

Lying in a giant field of grass, counting shooting stars

One day we'll all buy our vacation homes on Mars

With Nike gravity boots

And Tom Ford space suits that come in camouflage

But as for now, we wander overpriced department stores

What are we looking for inside the mall?

Last week I found a black hole beneath a pile of clothes at Ross
I fell in and got lost
Woke up four hours later in a discount suit from Boss
I keep it hanging on the hanger, hanging out with moths
Just another mediocre metaphor collecting moss

Tomorrow isn't promised to any of us

We're living in a dream even when we're waking up

Besides, it's not about us
It's about our *stuff*

So every moment should be special occasion enough

Now

Have you ever been excited for *Now*?

Well how about *Now*?

If not, just look around
Our feet are on the ground but we're standing upside down
The world is really round
And gravity is not the only force that holds us down
See, light is faster than the speed of sound
And outer space doesn't make a sound
Our inner space can be way more profound
I could say more, but how?
I'd be better off attempting to express it through a *howwwwl*

Everything is beautiful
Even when it's ugly

I know that seems unusual to almost everybody

So it's lucky you're not everybody

You're somebody

And the sum of anybody in a prehistoric body

So jump without the net

I promise you'll remember what you came here to forget

Have you ever been excited for *Now?*

Well how about *Now?*

Or *Now?*
Or *Now?*
Or even *Now?*

If not, just look around
Life is in HD
You get to be, taste, touch, hear, smell, see
You get to think free
No one controls your mind
You get to know yourself
You know that you can't be confined
You draw outside the lines
The lines were never there
I failed geometry but fit a circle in a square
I do not dim my shine
I do not even care
No one controls my mind
I can go anywhere

I can be anything as long as I can pay the price
So I don't cut myself and then go blame the fucking knife

I cannot live your life
And yet I'll give you mine
I have an open heart
You're welcome anytime

So how about *Now*?

Now? Or even *Now*?

Now could be good too

It all depends on you

Me?
I look around
The sun is shining bright
The birds are chirping in surround sound, out of sight
The wind is at my back
The clouds are rolling by
The trees are swaying and the grass is growing toward the sky

I am excited for *now*
For *now,* it's all I see

I am excited for *now*
I'm glad you're here with me

Sunset

You're so beautiful

the sunset

watches

you

Metamorphosis

Once there was a bird who fell in love with a fish

He was flying over the ocean doing flips and little tricks
He soared up high into the sky, then turned and did a dip
Falling fast into the water, he decided he'd get wet
So he took a breath and dove into the deepest, darkest blue
But underneath the sea
He did something he wouldn't normally do
He opened up his eyes, for the first time in his life
Then he looked around until he grew accustomed to the light
He saw a thousand shapes and colors
Swimming in and out of sight
He saw the flora dancing weightless
To the shallow beams of white
He had never known this world, yet somehow it felt right
Like it was home all along and he'd been visiting the skies

Then suddenly there was a flash
From the corner of his widened eyes

He saw a fish swim past

She was beautiful to his surprise

So graceful in the vast

She floated differently than him

But he recognized her path

Maybe she could teach him how to swim

There weren't words to ask

And yet they stopped to say hello

They circled slow, then fast

Mirroring where each other would go

He knew it couldn't last

But the moment was eternity

And though his breath was failing him

He had no will to turn and leave

He wanted to scream out

He longed to fly beneath the seas

The fish was nodding now

Apparently she too agreed

To swim amidst the clouds

With you is where I want to be

She said this without sound

They were sharing a collective dream

He felt his lungs press
He felt his heart compress
His head was saying *no*
His body saying *yes*
He reached for one caress
Then sprinted toward the surface
He shot into the sky and yet the air he got was worthless
He quickly turned, it took him merely seconds to return
Yet his love had disappeared, it was a slow and painful burn

Years passed, searching for the one that got away
He scoured every ocean, every stream, and every lake
He even doubled back just in case he'd made mistakes
But she was gone without a trace
So his soul ached for his soulmate

He was close to giving up
He landed on an island and collapsed, exhausted from his trip
And as the tide turned, he thought about his lost relationship
And he mourned, until his wings transformed into fins
Beak into gills, feathers into scales, all around
His skin was translucent, he was flopping on the ground
But then a wave came and lifted him into the sea
It's like the ocean wanted him enough to set him free

And as if on cue, she emerged from out the blue
He had flown around the world
But never seen such a view

She was gorgeous
Fly in the endless abyss
He was high, see, no sky could ever compare to this

He swam over clumsily, she greeted him with a kiss
Somehow their love had been a catalyst
For metamorphosis

And if I had to sum it up, I'd say that's what the moral is

He became what he *was*, because she loved what he *is*

See, it's true that a bird can fall in love with a fish

But eventually they're gonna have to find a place to live

When It's Right

Falling in love is like finding a home
In the heart of a person that you've never known

It's the waiting for the ring of the phone when you're alone
Or making them a playlist of all your favorite songs

Remember how it felt?
When their touch made you melt
When their presence made you a better version of yourself
When your bed was like an island in the middle of the sea
And their eyes were the only sunset you could see
When their smile was enough to inspire a forever
In this lifetime of learning how to love each other better

It is beyond words
It is knowing how she takes her tea
It is knowing when to challenge her and when to let her be
It is knowing when to hold her and when to set her free

It is chemistry and honesty, empathy, integrity and humility
It is calling when I'm gonna be late
Or giving her the last bite of cake from my plate
It is going on vacation and walking along the beach
It is the sound that she makes when she laughs in her sleep
It is real, especially when it's hard
Because we have chosen to reveal who we really are
Beautiful with all our scars

She's like a sky of stars
I've never felt as infinite as when she's in my arms

I've never felt as intimate as when I'm in her charms
I'd never met someone and instantly knew I belonged
So now the songs on the radio are making more sense
And every rom-com movie seems more intense
I'm having dreams that I'm painting her a picket fence
Our kids are playing on the lawn, still in innocence
Picturesque in every sense
It's like a Norman Rockwell, it feels so real
A modern fairy tale with a pool and barbecue grill
We'll have a two-car garage
And every week she'll get a gift certificate
For one free foot massage

And when she's had a hard day, we'll go and walk it off
And when she's had a hard night, we'll get some Häagen-Dazs
We'll put our goals on a list and then we'll cross them off
I'll take some pics of our kids
Then print them up and make a Mother's Day collage
Or send her flowers, just because . . .

Her skin is the closest that I've been to God

See, love is a long ladder up to heaven
It's like a dance where you move apart
And then come back together
It is sunshine and stormy weather
Because you would never know the one
Unless you knew the other

And in the end you'll be old and gray
With a pair of rocking chairs and some Grand Marnier
Grandkids on a grand piano in the foyer
Photographs of your family filling the hallway
And everybody in the neighborhood will ask you for advice
So you'll slowly lean in, then you'll look around twice
Then you'll whisper real light like it's the secret to your life

When you know, you know
'Cause when it's right, it's right

Creation

The highest form of creation
That's what we're witnessing
Two artists coming together to make a human being

Out of nothing into everything
Soon enough she'll be crawling, grabbing
Getting into everything
And you will teach her everything you know
And she will be your everything
And everyone will know
And they'll stop you on the street
And comment everywhere you go
About how beautiful she is
And you'll just nod in agreement at the miracle of it

You never really knew a love like this could exist, total bliss
Little hands, little feet, little head, look how little she is!
And yet she has the universe inside of every fingerprint
Rocking back and forth, singing to her softly as you sit

With your morning cup of coffee on an IV drip

Give her a gentle kiss, then watch her fall asleep on your chest

And let her body rise and fall with every grateful, deep breath

See, your heart is at rest

So even though your hair is a mess and you're sleepless

You have a purpose that is greater than your spouse, or yourself

Or your job, or your wealth, or even your health

You'd sacrifice it all if it would help to give her heaven over hell

And that drives you to excel

There is no more option to fail, the wind is at your sails

And since everything is new to her, it's new to you too

What is this? What is that? Who are they?

Peekaboo!

It's the wonder and amazement

Of the daily things she learns to do

And every lesson learned you get to live vicariously through

First step

First word

First smile

First tooth

Shoot, she'll have you wrapped around her finger

Before she turns two

Out of nothing into everything

Soon enough she'll be walking, talking, getting into everything

And she will teach you everything she knows

And she'll think that she knows everything

And she will tell you so

So even though you know she doesn't

You will give her the room to grow

But you will also give her boundaries so she knows how far to go

And know occasionally you might even have to use the word

No!

Take away her privileges or God forbid her cell phone

And she'll argue because parents just don't understand

They never have and never will

She'll slam the door and test your will

Like you don't pay the f'n bills

Hustle up her daily meals

Carpool from school to sports practice fields

She has some nerve to act this ill

That's when it hits you, this is how your parents used to feel

And you appreciate them for the first time, for real

This won't be easy

Nothing worth it ever is

But the love will always outweigh the momentary stress

And when they're at their worst, you will learn to be your best

And when they're at their best, it will balloon inside your chest

Until it fills you up, impressed, that you could ever be this blessed

You created art that's creating art with every breath

And if that's not success, our definition needs to switch

And if that's not rich, our definition needs to switch

And if that's not God, our definition needs to switch

Because honestly, this feeling is as good as it can ever get

Out of nothing into everything

Soon enough she'll be

Driving, dating, graduating

Leaving, living, working, mating

Getting into everything

Until eventually she's rocking an engagement ring

Then she'll get married and the cycle will begin again

You'll get to be a grandparent on the other end

And that is all life is

Our human trip is just a circle between birth and death

That's why above all else

We need to celebrate the now because it's precious

Take a bunch of pictures, but experience the present

And make sure that you listen, as a parent and a friend

Then again, that's just my advice . . .

But I don't have kids

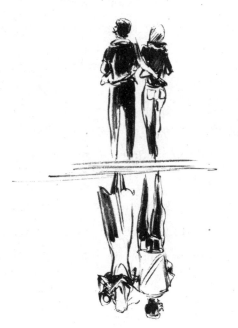

Flowers

One day

my future wife

will send you flowers

for your part in making me a better man

And you will deserve them

Break-Up

Many years ago, after a difficult break-up, I found myself sitting in front of my computer, attempting to write another break-up poem. Unfortunately, this had become a tradition for me. I wanted to describe in detail the anguish I was going through, so that others could learn from my mistakes. At least that's what I told myself. But for whatever reason, this time, before I began, I had the sudden desire to read over all of my old break-up poems first. I'm embarrassed to admit there were nine of them. So I sat on my couch, alone, in my dimly lit apartment, and read them, in a row, out loud, without stopping. Almost thirty minutes of material about relationships that hadn't worked out. When I finally finished, I shook my head in disbelief. All of my old break-up poems were applicable to my current break-up. It was in that moment that I realized, I didn't need to write a new break-up poem. I needed to figure out why I was continuing to create the same lesson in a different disguise over and over again.

Lessons

You can't learn a lesson
until you apply it to your life

That's why you can understand a lesson
and still have to learn it twice

Me?

I've learned the same lesson
more times than I would have liked

But the experience was priceless
so I had to pay the price

Change

Most people don't change

I mean they *won't* change

I mean they *can* change

But usually they *can't* seem to change

I find it so strange

People just continue to repeat similar patterns

Like the consequences don't matter, when they clearly do

What if God put a magnifying glass over you?

Over me?

Over everything we see?

And this world is an experiment for your soul

To survive separated from our infinite whole

I wouldn't know joy, unless I knew pain

I'm searching for a new way to say the same old thing

They say the same old thing, and then expect a different response

It's hard to explain, I guess the heart wants what it wants

I used to think I was right or wrong
Now I know I was wrong, so I write
Darkness is a form of light

I used to think I was mad at you
I was really mad at me
But in retrospect, that's how it had to be

I used to think I knew some shit
Now I know I don't know shit
But at least I know enough shit
To know I don't know shit

I'm a hitchhiking ghost trying to find his way home
Every mistake that I make I put inside of a poem

She wants to change her man, but she's focused on her man
She should focus on herself, rearrange her mental health

He wants to change his girl, but he's focused on his girl
He should focus on himself, rearrange his mental health

We wanna change the world, but we're focused on the world
We should focus on ourselves, why do I repeat myself?

Everybody's superpower doubles as their kryptonite

I think too much to sleep at night

But that's what makes me rip the mic

Seasons

If I could be the forest
I wouldn't judge the seasons
If all my leaves fell
I wouldn't analyze the reasons
I'd bend to every storm
But cling to every root
I'd be a thousand years old
And still be in my youth

Insomnia

One year for my birthday, a friend of mine gave me a gift certificate for a Reiki session at a holistic clinic in Malibu. I'd been having so much trouble sleeping that I was hooked on Xanax, and she thought this might be the solution to my chronic insomnia. I had no idea what Reiki was, but I'm a sucker for spirituality, so I set up the appointment. When I arrived, the self-proclaimed healer met me in the reception area. She was from England. We sat down and she asked me a few general questions about my life. I answered suspiciously. She then explained that Reiki is a form of energy healing that can improve the life flow of the patient and help to bring their chakras into perfect alignment. I didn't know what that meant, but I followed her into the room, undressed, and laid down on the massage table. She lit candles, turned on ambient music and put a lavender-scented blindfold over my eyes. I could hear her rubbing her hands together like Mr. Miyagi before cracking Daniel's leg back into place. I could sense her hovering over different parts of my body and even felt the heat from our energy exchange. After a few minutes, I drifted off into what I can only describe as a daydream. I vaguely remember being a mouse running through blades of grass on a hot summer day. An hour later, I awoke from my sleep and sat up to find her holding my feet, crying.

"Are you okay?" I asked.

She sat down.

"Sorry," she said. "This rarely ever happens to me."

"What?"

"I was just really moved by our session."

She was still holding my feet.

"Oh," I said.

"Can I tell you something?"

"Sure," I said.

"You have so much love to give," she whispered.

I didn't respond.

"But you've hidden all of your hurt behind this tough exterior, and during our session I could hear your heart, and it was literally screaming to get out."

She started crying again.

"Okay, well . . . thanks. I appreciate that," I said. "I really do."

We sat there for another ten seconds.

"Should I put my clothes back on now?"

Inquire Within

I used to look up when I prayed
I would raise my head to the sky
As if God lived in a penthouse made of clouds

As a kid
I thought he could hear my prayers better when I was on a plane
After all, I was closer to him
I would ride elevators to the top floor
Just to whisper my secret desires

I've never told anyone that

As an adolescent I stopped praying altogether
I didn't believe in belief
It seemed to me that people had created God
To control themselves and others
It was the long con
Self-delusion as a form of therapy
I convinced myself I was stronger than that

I wasn't

As a young man I explored spirituality
I wanted **answers**
I devoured every self-help book I could get my hands on
I watched *The Secret* two times in a row
And still somehow managed to misunderstand
The law of attraction
It was quite comical, really

They say the difference between
Intelligence and wisdom is experience
But you can have experience
Without having wisdom or intelligence
So what the fuck do they know?

Recently I started praying again

I couldn't specifically tell you why, but if pressed . . .
I'd say it had to do with a sudden
And unexpected need to surrender

I felt the urge to bow in the service
Of something greater than myself
But I didn't want religion to get in the way

So one night, as the overwhelming silence of the city

Filled my empty room

I knelt at the foot of my bed and I prayed

It was oddly familiar

Except this time

Instead of looking *up* to God

I looked inside

Perspective

It's not enough
To make my dreams come true
I wanna enjoy them as I do
'Cause you can climb
The highest mountaintop
And never change your view

Whistle

This one time, I saw a dude who worked for Vons
Collecting stacks of shopping carts in the parking lot
With only one arm

Now I should say that on this particular day
I had been feeling down about myself
Depressed about some stupid shit
Complaining in my head
That I'm not as far along as I would like to be
That life is victimizing me

And mind you, I was buying food at the time

To put into my car, to put into my house

To put into my fridge, to put into my mouth

And that's when I saw him

Ten carts deep

Pushing them with one arm down the street, whistling

Now I swear, he was whistling

Do you know how happy I would have to be

To spontaneously pucker up my lips

Like I was about to blow a kiss

Then open up a bit

And push some hot air from my larynx into a higher pitch?

Shit

Really, fucking, happy

Anyway, back to this dude

The first thought I had, I'll admit, was a bit rude

But hear me out before you boo

See, I was confused

'Cause if I was in his shoes and I had to choose a job

This would not be the job I'd choose

And I know that sounds hard-core

But honestly

This is one of the jobs that I would want two arms for

Now that being said

This particular dude was an absolute gangster

The arm he had looked like it was strong enough

To be the anchor on an oil tanker

Like he could've been Arnold Schwarzenegger's trainer

Back when he was starring in *The Terminator*

And it woke me up like the scent from a cup of sencha

So I went home and wrote this poem as an ode to thank him

It really got me thinking about my situation

Why the hell am I complaining?

This world is full of people maintaining

No matter who you are or where you're from

We all have to wake up every day and accept the fact

That we don't know where we'll go, or why we've come

Which can cause confusion

So we distract ourselves and focus on amusement
Instead of self-improvement
A mutually agreed-upon collective delusion
But with this much stimulus and this little understanding
It's a wonder we don't all just completely fucking lose it

Genius and insanity are closer than they seem
Your perspective is the difference
Between your nightmares and your dreams

Because if everything is energy and my body is a vessel
Then my struggle is unique but that doesn't make it special

And this one-armed man had the strength to up and whistle
With a fistful of shopping carts that he guided like a missile
And it blew me away like a sneeze into a tissue
That someone who has seemingly so many issues
Could be unequivocally so blissful
While someone who's as lucky as I am
Could be self-creating problems by the list full

So from this point on

If my thoughts start thinking they're important
Or my feelings start feeling distorted

I'm gonna sort them into categories to see if I can change them

If I can, I'll simply make the moves to rearrange them

If I can't, I'll acknowledge them, but won't engage them

I'll gather all my confidence and courage as I face them and . . .

Whistle

The Last Laugh

Right before I die, I'm gonna tell a joke
So that everyone at my bedside can laugh before I croak
Most depart on somber notes, but life is serious enough
And we take our seriousness so serious, for what?
Just because we're serious, doesn't mean we're tough
It requires more courage to laugh when times get rough
Because laughter doubles as an outlet when energy is stuck
It can disrupt

A pattern
Long enough

To shift

How you
Look

And when you shift

How you look

You shift how
You
Look

That way people see you differently and it changes shit up
The glass is either half empty
Or half filled up
I'm just grateful that I have a cup

So many brag about how they don't give a fuck
Because they have no fucks to give
Me? I give so many fucks that you'd think I'd have none left
But my fucks are exponential, so I'll give until my death
'Cause I'll have infinite fucks until my very last breath
And that's when I'll tell my joke

And it will be sooooo gooood
That the waiting room will laugh
Like they never knew they could
And they'll have to tell their friends
And their friends will laugh too
And pretty soon the whole city will be laughing at the truth

And they'll laugh until they cry

And they'll cry until they scream

And they'll scream until they love

And they'll love until they dream

It was just a little joke, I didn't know what it could mean

It was just a little joke, now the joke is on me

Because the laughter was contagious, so it spread across the land

My punch line was so outrageous, people couldn't even stand

They started rolling on the floors

They started giving up beliefs

They started begging me for more

But I was already deceased

It didn't matter, rich or poor

Forget the languages they speak

Because the heart can understand

So it rippled through the streets

And they laughed beyond their fears

And they laughed beyond their grief

And they laughed beyond their wars

They laughed themselves right into peace

We are pieces in a puzzle but we've never seen the box

We're addicted to the struggle, it's a fucking paradox

But I put that in my joke

So the irony was obvious

A deathbed roast

My clarity was so hilarious that everybody choked

Then they laughed about the choking

It was universal dope, and humanity was smoking

They were high on their emotions

Overwhelmed by their devotion

They heard the laughter coming

From the mountains and the oceans

They heard the laughter coming from the skies and trees

Even the universe was laughing as it fell to its knees

And right then the laughter stopped

It was almost all at once

At first it was a shock, the transition was abrupt

But eventually they settled in, united in their work

They had a lot to do together as they built a better earth

I never saw it happen, but I was praying that it did

I held my wife and kids' hands as I closed my eyelids

And I dreamt about this world and the things we could create

If I could find the right joke before my soul evacuates

So I opened up my mouth, but I had nothing left to say

So my joke was in the silence, as I slowly slipped away . . .

Silence

It took me my whole life to write that poem

Reincarnation

When I die

I imagine that it will be like waking up from a long dream
I'll stretch my arms and look around at all that was unseen
A world beyond the world our five senses perceive
My identity will be gone, yet somehow I'll feel relieved
It's always gotten in the way of the connection that I crave
Now that everything is energy I gladly ride the wave
It's easier when you don't have a self, you never misbehave
Plus you never have to do the simple stuff like shit and shave
And you never have to worry about the money you didn't save
Up here everything is free
And the moment is what pays
See, without the world of form
There is nothing to protect
Everyone is one
So love is not something that you project
It is all there is

Life was made to marvel at itself

I see that now that I don't have to play the cards I was dealt

Wow, this place is so serene, it's ideal in every way

I can manifest ideas out of formless balls of clay

But since thoughts become reality, there's nothing to convey

So I'm silent to myself throughout my nonexistent day

And infinity is watching when I close my eyes to pray

'Cause even God prays to God as crazy as that is to say

Plus I'm not confined to time, therefore I'm early when I'm late

Because my body has no boundaries for my spirit to escape

I am everywhere at once, undefined by any shape

The only rule I have is don't consume more than you can create

See, when you die you download your hard drive and get erased

You become the empty space

And your memories and dreams echo endlessly in space

A collective clean slate

Life can only transform, it can never be replaced

And from this view, I look at you and think

It's fun to watch you chase

Secretly, sometimes I even wish that I could take your place

I kinda miss the ups and downs

All the triumphs and mistakes

The science of the human state

There's a language to the universe

And most times, it takes us lifetimes to translate

Then we can learn to speak our fate

To compassionately love or to compassionately hate

But the dichotomy is vast so the suffering is great

We don't remember life's a mask so we're dying to escape

And we're living to escape

And the pressure gets so heavy we don't even wanna wait

Getting crushed under the weight

We're so impatient that we try to bust the lock on heaven's gate

But there is no lock on heaven's gate

There is no line, there is no wait

There is no list for us to make

There's only bliss, and only grace

And knowing this is kind of laced

I wanna borrow someone's face

I wanna have amnesia too

So I can take the ride like you

And in an instant I'm being pushed into the light

I almost fit, but not quite

I hear a woman scream and fight

I try to help with all my might

The doctors pull me into life

I open up my eyes to sight
The room is big and bright and white
The nurses clean me with a wipe
They label me a gender type
I can't remember why I came
And then I hear her say my name

And suddenly I feel an overwhelming calm

They wrap me in a blanket and place me in her loving arms

And for a moment I'm alive and I know I belong

I look into her eyes and once again I meet my mom

The New You

You're not going through it, it's going through you
And once it's all gone, you'll become the new you
With a different perspective from the same point of view
Fully unaffected by the old truth you once knew
Connected at the roots, to the trunk, to the branches
To the leaves and the way they fly away in wind dances
A frantic seesaw, free-fall in midair
That represents the floating folly
Of us all being here

The Weather

You can't argue with the weather

It just makes you look stupid

You can't convince a storm not to rain on your parade

But you can buy an umbrella

What you can't do

Is give the sun a guilt treatment for not showing up

It doesn't work that way

You can't yell loud enough for the clouds to care

They're not here for you

You can't reason with a tornado because you're dizzy

You can't negotiate with an avalanche

Or judge lightning for striking twice

Once I saw a guy complaining to the stars

Because they weren't bright enough to light his path

I had to swallow my laughter

Why are you debating with the wind

When you could just turn around and allow it to fill your sails?

You can't argue with the weather

Trust me

(

I've tried

Ideas and Ideologies

Recently, my *new* therapist and I were discussing the differences between ideas and ideologies. He was saying that ideas are tools that you can use in your life that will change as your truth and your experience change. Ideologies, on the other hand, are like prisons that you have to force your reality into; otherwise you will lose control over that ideology, and that part of your life.

This resonated deeply with me, because I use far too many ideologies, whether they were handed down to me, or I created them myself. So as I was walking back to my car, I thought, from now on, I am only going to use ideas. I decided to repeat this out loud as a declaration to the universe.

"From now on, I am only going to use ideas!"

But then I thought
Shit . . . I just created a new ideology.

Evidence

You will always find the evidence for what you choose to believe

You will always find the evidence for what you choose to believe

Starve your pain, find your ego
Starve your ego, find your beast
Starve your beast, find your truth
Find your truth, find your peace

You will always find the evidence for what you choose to believe

You will
always
find
the evidence
for what
you choose
to believe

You
will
always
find
the
evidence
for
what
you
choose
to
believe

So if you don't like your story

Don't believe it

Then leave

Learned Fear

Learned fear can be overcome when you realize
The voice inside your head is not yours
It's an imitation of the voices from before
Repeating on a loop inside your quiet core
Receiving since your youth
When your choices weren't even yours
Perceiving was the proof, but reality has many doors

So why are we still fighting other people's wars?

Learned fear can be overcome when you realize
The voice inside your head is not yours
It's an imitation of the voices from before
Repeating on a loop inside your quiet core
And you can't tell the difference, because it sounds the same
But trust me when I tell you
Most of what you think is from somebody else's brain

They have us trained
Shackled by imaginary chains
Imaginary rules for imaginary games
But they don't know the reasons either
So where should we place the blame?
And who is *they* anyway, when we're all the same?

Our parents had parents
And their parents had parents
Apparently it hurts to see
So I'll be transparent

The world is so much bigger than your insecurities
And they don't speak on your behalf
Without your soul's authority
The world is so much bigger than your culture or community
And they don't speak on your behalf
Without your soul's authority

Because if it's all a story, then nobody else can tell it for me
Since I'm always transforming, I defy a category
When you do the same thing, the same way, it's habit forming
But nothing in this land of mortal man is mandatory
We're all just transitory

Your life's a laboratory

Experimenting on today can change tomorrow morning

And since matter

is

mostly

e   m   p   t   y

space

We're in a sea of consciousness, where the boundaries **are** erased

So I stared at my reflection, until I couldn't see my face

Then I picked myself and put the flowers in an empty vase

If you came for validation then you're in the wrong place

The only certain satisfaction is becoming what you've chased

And there's no running from the inner voice

So it's important that you choose

But it's more important that you know you have a choice

You have a choice

Are you living someone else's life?

You have a voice

Does it haunt you in the dead of night?

Would you fly if you weren't convinced to be afraid of heights?

And who convinced you anyway?
They had no fucking right

Right?

No one can steal your light
You shine within so bright
That you could blind the sun from sight
And scare him back into the night

No one can steal your light
I said it twice because you're greater than the circumstances
That surround your perfect life

You're not your nature or your nurture, you're a prototype
And if you hone it right, eventually you'll hack your satellite

At first it's nothing
Then nothing turns into a whisper
Turn the dial and it gets crisper in your transistor
Wait a while
And the whisper turns into a scream

It overwhelms your system and you won't know what it means

But pump the volume up and it can tell you all your dreams
Till pretty soon it's the only voice you'll ever need
Now all you have to do is listen when you want to lead
Your fear disintegrates when you decide to stop, and breathe

It's *your* authentic voice
No matter where you go, it never leaves

And that's God no matter what religion you believe

My Religion

I'm starting my own religion

And everyone is welcome

But nobody can join

If you did, you'd miss the point

Keep Loving

Keep loving through your sadness

Keep loving through your fears

Keep loving through your anger

Kcep loving through your tears

Keep loving through your failure

Keep loving through success

Keep loving through anxiety

Keep loving through your stress

Keep loving through rejection

Keep loving through mistrust

Keep loving through your jealousy

Keep loving through your lust

Keep loving through your shallow

Keep loving through your depth

Keep loving until loving is the only thing that's left

85

I wanna fall in love at 85

Go on shuffleboard dates and dance to hip-hop from '95
We'd also listen to the song "Stayin' Alive"
But only for the message
Otherwise we'd keep away from disco, it's depressing
We'd rock matching tracksuits and rope gold chains
We'd look like Run DMC, but in their old age
We'd take aerobics classes and wear bifocal glasses
And eat at IHOP and hold hands at Sunday masses
And when it comes to the bedroom?

Well, nothing much would happen in the bedroom
Because we're 85

But we would still be down to take a walk, or take a drive
Or sit and talk, and have a drink
Watch the passersby, and ask each other why
And how, and who, and where, and when

And then we'd laugh and cry again
About the people we had been
And I would touch her withered skin
And comment on how thin it is
To keep in something infinite

And she would smile sweet and blush
Then tell me that I think too much
She's right, I think too much
It's always been a problem
But then again, that's how I made my green like the Goblin
When I was in my twenties, I was eating Top Ramen
Counting up my pennies, saving up to go food shopping
But now I'm 85, and somehow I feel more alive!
I turn my hearing aid up and bump Jurassic 5
I read the sports page while she peruses classifieds
We like antique stores, garage sales, and barter buys

And when it comes to the bedroom?

Well hopefully, every once in a while

She lets me knock her boots
Into the floral patterns of our bedpost
Then hold her head close, like death isn't chasing us

Planning on erasing us, and replacing us

With better versions of us

Reshaping us, remaking us

Then recreating us, with new identities

So we can make new memories

Hush, little baby

Learn to walk, and talk, and think, and lie

And feel, and fight, and love, and die

And never get the answers why

She dips a joint of grass in wheatgrass and we get high

Her hair is silver as the moon in the Miami sky

We still pop pills

But it's not the Molly anymore

Whenever we can't sleep we listen to the ocean floor

She got a sounds-of-the-sea CD for me from the Brookstone store

And ever since I've been snoring like a . . .

Like a really good metaphor for snoring!

Sorry, I go blank sometimes. What? I'm 85!

I'm not complaining, I'm just happy that I'm still alive

And happy that I have my better half by my side

Super fly, she doesn't look a day over 75

When I first saw her, I was totally in awe

She was classical, so I was like, "Yo-Yo Ma"

And that was all it took, a single look and I was shook
I fell for her like some loose shingles from our Spanish roof
And I will love her till she loses every last root
And has to glue dentures to her gums to chew solid food

Ooooh

Now that's real love, dude

That's some push comes to shove love

Not when it's convenient love

Hospital bed love

Feed her ice chips love

Never leave the room love

Sleeping in the chair love

Pray to up above love

Have to pull the plug love

Miss her in my bones love

Everything about her love

Die within a month love

Can't live without her love

Love, the only reason that we're alive

And none of us should have to wait until we're 85

PART TWO
EXHALE

What If

What if Martin Luther King Jr. was into video games?

What if Gandhi liked to Netflix and chill?

What if Einstein was on Prozac?

What if Buddha was too stressed to sit still?

What if Mother Teresa counted likes, instead of counting hugs?
What if Cleopatra was a supermodel
Who spent her nights in clubs?

What if Socrates was a contestant on *The Bachelorette*?
What if Rumi was in advertising, would I buy his shit?

What if Rosa Parks missed the bus and couldn't take a Lyft?
What if Bob Marley popped barbiturates
Instead of puffing spliffs?

What if TMZ had followed JFK?

What if Lincoln was a backup center in the NBA?

What if John Lennon sang "Imagine" on *American Idol*?

Would they wanna add a beat, get a feature, change the title?

What if Muhammad Ali had a reality show?

What if I got my house painted by Picasso or Van Gogh?

What if Churchill had a podcast? Or Disney liked to scroll?

What if Shakespeare drove an Uber?

Would thou knowest I was home?

What if Dali was a DJ? Or Tupac never rapped?

What if Malcolm was your ex? Or Mandela made the latest app?

What if Che Guevara had a clothing line?

Or Frida Kahlo made the logos for their marketing team?

What if Jane Austen wrote scripts for shitty sitcoms?

Or Steve Jobs did social media targeting for all your moms?

What if Bruce Lee taught Zumba, not Jeet Kune Do?

What if he didn't ever do what he was destined to do?

What if our heroes aren't demigods to look up to?

What if our heroes are our heroes
'Cause they're just like me and you?

What if I just sit inside this room and wait to die?
What if I try to change the world and fail?
At least I tried

I could numb myself a hundred ways to hypnotize my soul
So much unfulfilled potential you would think it was my goal

What are you doing with your time?
Yours
And mine?

What if our next genius artist, activist, or inventor
Grows up to wanna be an Instagram influencer?

What are you doing with your time?
Yours
And mine?

You don't wanna have regrets for all the years you've left behind
And every year that passes someone's coming up behind

They're here to take our place, in a never-ending line

So what's your higher purpose and is it worth the grind?
It's gonna take some hard work
You have to burn before you shine

Are your thoughts

And your dreams

And your actions

All aligned?

What are you doing with your . . .

Superpowers

When I think of superheroes, I think of superhuman
I think of Superman, Black Panther, and Wonder Woman

Usually they have a cape or a mask to hide their face
They have X-ray vision and superhuman strength
Some can even breathe in outer space
They fly around awhile
But always come back to keep our cities safe

They're here to save humanity from itself
It's a metaphor for how we look outside ourselves for help
And while the fantasies are fun, I choose to look to me and you
Yeah, we love superheroes, but we have superpowers too

It starts with being open to this moment
If you do, then you can own it
Besides, it'll be gone before you know it, so don't blow it
You owe it to this second of eternity to show up
Embrace the possibilities and slow up

Take a breath
Look around
See the sights
Hear the sounds
Feel the ground
Notice how the gravity weighs you down

You could be anywhere and yet you're here
When you embrace it as your own
You begin to overcome your fears

And real courage is staring in the mirror
It's deciding what you want to do, then making it appear
It's creating out of thin air
You must be doing something right if you got scared
Otherwise you wouldn't care

It's a process to get from here to there
You're on the journey and you're learning
But building muscle means you're gonna feel some burning
So don't deny it, simplify it, try it, see if it can work for you
Shift perspective to get a different view
And don't forget you gotta laugh at the truth
'Cause sometimes a sense of humor
Is the only thing that pulls us through

It's medicine when you can let it in

An attitude of gratitude will bubble up from within

So even when the storm clouds block the blue from your sky

You'll remember that the sun is waiting for you on the other side

And having fun is something we must decide

From the lows to the highs, it's all a part of the ride

I can throw my hands up or hold on for dear life

But I'd rather live once than have to go to hell twice

Compassion is my passion

Empathy is my gift

But my growth is incremental

As my consciousness shifts

So I create from the abyss, turning pain into gold

I'm an alchemist, an optimist, and an authentic soul

I believe that life is good
Even when it hurts to see

I believe in superpowers
And I believe in you and me

I believe in superheroes
But I don't look for them above

Because they exist **inside** us all
And we save the day with love

Bipartisan

I've been dating a Republican, it's crazy but it's true.
And if we can make it work, America, so can you!

She believes in smaller government, trickle-down economics,
and job creators doing what they've promised.

I believe in universal health care. That billionaires should pay
their fair share for the opportunities it took to get them here.
A little here, a little there, can help to go a long way for people
who are day to day in poverty, and possibly, that philosophy
could start to rebuild a middle class that's been slowly decimated
in the past twenty years, mostly 'cause of corporate greed being
more important to our politicians than the voters' needs.

"Oh my God, Adam, that's naive but it's cute. If our taxes help
poor people, show me where's the proof. Governmental subsidies
are just a socialist excuse not to produce, and keep communities
in a dependence loop. Our citizens should take responsibility for

what they do, instead of trying to blame all their problems on me or you."

"Hmm, that's kinda true, I guess I'll give you that, but you're not taking education into consideration in this conversation, or the history of institutionalized racism, or the drug laws that put people into paid prisons, or the way religion has been used as a division. I just think you're missing why the government might need to step in, assess the situation that we're facing, and provide a social safety net for changing it. Americans deserve to have an equal chance at making it!"

"Yeah, but not by taking it. And why are you yelling!?"

"I'm not yelling, I'm just passionate! I'm trying to get us on the same page like an asterisk."*

"Well, you should dial it back a bit, 'cause your facts are inaccurate, and when you act like this, it just, ugh, gets me so pissed! I mean it's only common sense, look at how the Congress spends! Obamacare has brought us right up to the fiscal cliff, we need to get a grip, before complete collapse, loosen up the regulations and reduce the tax, I'm just reporting facts."

"Yeah, according to Fox News perhaps, fair and balanced my ass! The only stats that they count is cash, by perpetuating fear for commercial revenue, and pushing Rupert Murdoch's right-wing agenda through our living rooms. How can we debate when your side refuses compromise, and peddles lies, even at the risk of our complete demise, then blames us for being un-American, when they rejected every fucking bill we've tried, and we're supposed to sacrifice?"

"You're yelling again, can you please lower your voice? This is not a competition over who can make the loudest noise. We've both made some valid points, and at the very least we agree on legalizing pot, equal rights, and pro-choice. It's like you think I'm a bad person."

"I'm not saying you're a bad person."

"It seems like you're saying I'm a bad person."

"Baby, I'm certain you're a great person. That's why you're all up in my head like a brain surgeon. And usually you have me wrapped around your finger like a sea urchin. Seriously though,

I'm sorry for the fucking cursing. Politics turns me into an
insane person."

I pause and wait for a response
She stares at me with crossed arms
She leans in for a little kiss
I pucker up my puny lips

"You wanna watch some Fox News? I promise not to blow a fuse."

"How about we watch some BBC, that way it's neither you or me."

She crawls into my open arms
I hold her close and all is calm

"You know I love you even when you're wrong. But you should never, *ever* try to have this conversation with my mom."

*We broke up

Problems

How do we talk about the problems without feeding them?

If we ignore them, we most likely keep repeating them

If we explore them, we run the risk of reinforcing them

So how then do we get down to the source of them?

Dear White Americans

Imagine if the roles were reversed
And white people were enslaved by black people first

And for almost 300 years they forced us into work
And they beat us, raped us, and tortured us
And then they went to church
And they treated us like dirt
And they chained us, and they whipped us
And they told us we were cursed
And they sold us on the auction blocks like that was what we're worth
And they outlawed us to read, or write, or vote
But what was worse
They would hang us by our necks
So that witnesses could look
And see our bodies slowly swaying from a tree like a fruit

Imagine what that took
If generations passed before the melting pot could cook
And our nation had to go to war before we closed the book

But freedom wasn't peaceful
It was as brutal as it looked
Segregation isolated us
Because of how we looked

And neighborhoods were separate
We educated separate
We congregated, dated, mated, ate, and drank separate
They made us travel separate
They made our toilets separate
The hospitals were separate
The telephones were separate
They made our pools separate
They made our parks separate
And when it wasn't separate they would split us into sections
So that they would get the best seats
While we would get the worst

I want you to imagine if the history reversed

That we were the ones terrorized by the Ku Klux Klan
And a pointy white hood hunted down the white man
And police would beat us daily without any repercussions
See, the justice system's blind, but only to its own corruption
So people started demonstrating, marching, and protesting

We couldn't take it any longer
We had had enough
And when enough people have enough
The people have the power
So a coalition joined the fight, but civil rights was ours
And the boycotts were ours
And the sit-ins were ours
And the riots were ours
And the leaders were ours
And when our leaders lost their lives, the grief was also ours
So we raised our fists in conscious militance to be empowered

And America was moving at a million miles an hour
But we'd taken strides politically, to even out the power
Now educated whites could become
Lawyers or professors
Doctors or directors
Bankers or investors
But mostly our jobs were still industrial in nature
So when they closed the factories, they didn't need our labor
And this affected more than just the money in our wallets
Because areas that once were working class became impoverished

Imagine how that felt
To be unable to provide

To look your children in the eyes without a 9 to 5
So families were broken
And neighborhoods were broken
And liquor stores were opened
And gun stores were opened
And drugs were on the rise, but the reasons were unspoken
And gangs were on the rise, but the reasons were unspoken
And while pop culture painted us as being dumb or dangerous
We struggled to survive inside a system that was blaming us
And still somehow we thrived out of all of that upheaval
To amplify the unheard voices of our people

But imagine all the unheard voices of our people

Imagine, if you didn't have to imagine, that you weren't treated equal

Imagine the resentment you might have against the system
If white males were disproportionately cycled into prisons
Imagine your aggression
If people were afraid of you because of your complexion
If strangers crossed the street when you were walking their direction
Just because of their suspicion
Imagine your suspicion
If when you talked about it, other races wouldn't listen

In fact they made you wrong for even bringing up oppression
Their perception was for you to stop acting like a victim

Imagine the disconnection

Then finally a white person wins the presidential election
And half the country celebrates this symbol of progression

But the other half is moving in the opposite direction
So the next president we elect is a blatant racist

We still have unacknowledged privilege
Still voting rights restrictions
Still biased cops on traffic stops, and widespread division
From those poverty stricken, to those making decisions

Still uneven nutrition
Underfunded education
Still job discrimination
Still home discrimination
Still loan discrimination
Still pay discrimination

Still dealing with that normal everyday discrimination

And Michael Brown was white

And Trayvon Martin was white

And Freddie Gray was white

And Eric Garner was white

And Oscar Grant was white

And Sandra Bland was white

And Stephon Clark was white

And so were countless others

Yet our country wants us to believe that racism is over

Protect and Serve

I don't know what it takes to put on a uniform
To risk your life for a stranger
To wake up every day and shield us from the danger
To protect and serve

But those are the words
To protect
And serve

To protect: "To keep safe from harm or injury"
To serve: "To perform duties or services for another person"

Does everyone feel protected?
Does everyone feel served?

Or do some people feel unsure, insecure, and unnerved?
When cops pass you on the streets are you harassed or disturbed?
Pulled over, pulled out of your car, and cuffed on the curb?

Did you fit the description?

Were you driving while black?
Were you walking while black?
Were you talking while black?
Were you breathing while black?
Were you living while black?

Were you unarmed and running when they shot you in the back?
Did your mother have a funeral?
Was everyone in black?
Was she crying at the coffin?
Did they have to hold her back?
Did they put you on a shirt?
Did they wear you on a hat?
Did your name become a hashtag when you were more than that?

Or maybe you were mourning someone close
But every pew was packed
So instead of sitting down, you wound up standing in the back
Did you know someone who died
For nothing more than being black?
Did you love someone who died for the crime of being black?
Are you scared of your protectors?

Do you think they might attack?
Did you have to tell your children how to speak and how to act?
Did you have to sit them down and explain the painful facts?
The uniforms are blue, but the bodies brown and black

Don't make any sudden moves, answer everything they ask
Don't raise your voice to make a point, you have to stay relaxed

These are survival skills beyond your economic class
These are survival skills if you're alive and you're black

If the sirens start flashing and you have to interact
Keep your hands on the wheel, keep your eyes on the dash
Only get your license and your registration when they ask
Don't put yourself in jeopardy for arguing while black
If you've done nothing wrong, it can escalate fast
If you reach for your phone or you ask for their badge

You don't wanna go viral for dying while black
You don't wanna be famous for dying while black

And you don't wanna watch the officer get off with a slap
When it's someone that *you love* and they're never coming back

I don't know what it takes to put on a uniform

To risk your life for a stranger

To wake up every day and shield us from the danger

To protect
And serve

Keep Loving: Part II

Keep loving through the violence

Keep loving through the hate

Keep loving through the silence

Keep loving through debate

Keep loving through confusion

Keep loving through regret

Keep loving through the madness

Keep loving through the mess

Keep loving through forgiveness

Keep loving through the threats

Keep loving through indifference

Keep loving through distress

Keep loving through the changes

Keep loving through the death

Keep loving until loving is the only thing that's left

Look Closer

Look closer

Behind every stranger is a person

The stories are different

But the journey is the same

We're too caught up on the places, or the faces, or the names

And when we focus on the differences, it's easier to blame

'Cause it's hard to see the picture

When you're hung up on the frame

America's a work of art because of struggle and pain

From the crowded city streets to the Rocky Mountain range

Our country is alive

And the spirit still remains

So the highways twist and turn across the map

Like they were veins

Connecting us together, even when we can't agree

'Cause our common ground

Is that we have the freedom to be free

To take responsibility for who we choose to be

To find a compromise between the things that we believe
Because despite our disagreements and the ways we've all felt

If you stop and look close enough
You might just see yourself

Citizens United

Hi

I'm a corporation

And I'm a person

So we can have a meeting, but we can't meet up in person

'Cause I don't have a body

I'm more of an idea

My living room's a lobby

My kitchen is a cafeteria

I'm a person though

I promise you I am

So we can make a deal

But you can't shake my hand

Because I'm not a man

I just have the rights of one

Doesn't matter what I do, as long as I can get it done

See, I don't have a soul

So I don't have to die

Which means I never have to ask myself the question why
The sky's the limit
While the smog is filling up the sky
I'd probably grimace
But I never grew a pair of eyes
See, I'm a corporation
But I'm a person too
And to the Supreme Court, I'm equally as real as you
So I can buy elections
And lobby for my cause
It's just a contribution
I'm not breaking any laws
And even if I did, there's no one here for them to blame
I've got a logo and a brand
I don't have a name
See, I'm a person, but a person has to feel the pain
So they can fine me and it's fine
I don't feel ashamed
I'll just fire someone
And then claim I never knew
Hand out a severance package
Then go hire someone new
I've heard that empathy can make a normal person pause

But I'm a corporation, so I'm greedy by the law

Which makes it easy to ignore the misery I've caused

'Cause my responsibility is to a higher cause

The market is my God

I prey, but on the weak

I have the loudest voice around

And yet I never speak

See, I'm a corporation, but I'm a person too

And there are people in this person that are just like you

Sometimes they're working in an office with a gorgeous view

Or in a basement maze of never-ending cubicles

I own a corporate jet

My home is where I land

How can I stand for anything?

I don't have legs to stand

I chill with Exxon, Monsanto, and Goldman Sachs

We sit around and laugh, while we count our countless stacks

We make up super PACs

I swear we rule the world

And yet we'll never have to raise a little boy or girl

We are the corporations
We are the people too

Except the people running us
Have us running you

Hollywood

El Pollo Loco has always been my favorite fast-food chain. It's inexpensive and arguably healthy, so whether you're on a budget, in a rush, or both, it's the perfect pick. In fact, in my younger, broker years, I survived almost solely on a diet of BRC burritos and tacos al carbon.

At the time, I had discovered a loophole in the El Pollo Loco system that allowed me to ask for extra beans, and extra rice, on a bigger tortilla, for no extra charge. They have since corrected this. I'd like to think that I am personally responsible for the change.

Anyway, occasionally when I had some extra money, I would splurge and order the half chicken meal, which came with two sides and full access to the salsa bar. This was very exciting. I would pile onions, cilantro, and pico de gallo as high as my Styrofoam plate could carry. On one such occasion, after finishing my lunch, I had put some leftover rice in a to-go container. As I walked outside, I passed a homeless guy, who asked if I had any change.

"You know, I actually don't have any change," I said, "but I'd be happy to give you the rest of this rice."

"Naw, that's cool man," he said. "I'm trying not to eat carbohydrates."

Only in Hollywood, I thought.

But then I thought, *only in America*.

America

"I'm about to buy a bunch of shit that I don't need.

What? I got a credit card, I can afford these.

Ima getta better car.

Ima getta bigger house.

Ima getta iPhone 20.

Ima getta leather couch.

Ima getta gym membership that I won't use.

Ima pop prescription pills and drink booze.

Ima cop my girl fake boobs.

Ima getta pair of baby alligator shoes and a three-piece suit."

"I'm a legend in my own mind!

I'm 'bout to stick a wind turbine in a coal mine.

I got a fat gut and a George Foreman grill.

I got a MacBook loading up my acting reel.

I got a pool that I never clean.

I'll take a Hummer limousine to the Everglades

Hunt with an M16 and kill everything.

I got a barbed-wire tattoo because it looks menacing.
I leave the house with the lights on.
My favorite part of the day is feeding mice to my python."

"I don't believe global warming exists.
It's a myth, scientists have invented the shit.
And I admit there's some climate differences, but that's it.
It's just a normal planetary shift.
Dude, get a grip.
I drive a Mustang so my mustache is a must-have.
I wear a musk that is made from a muskrat's nutsack.
I have a Snuggie, two pending lawsuits
And a daughter thin enough to Hula-Hoop a Froot Loop.
I pick up my wife's dog's Pomeranian poop.
My therapist has a therapist, so it's like a whole support group.
See, I'm pro-life and I'm pro-death-penalty
And essentially the pressure has been messing with me mentally.
God tell me what to do.
I know that no one is as hypocritical as you.
Isn't that true?"

"Oooooh, we should get some new shoes.
Let's hit the mall, y'all.
Shop until we feel used.

I want it all.

Call Janie tell her where we are.

Well screw it, she can just record it on her DVR.

I'll text her from the car.

But bring me Xanax

Cuz Amber's dating Xander and it's making me all manic.

I saw them at the Standard, getting hammered, and I panicked.

I just don't understand it.

He's taking me for granted.

I haven't felt this bad since I saw the Titanic.

And to be perfectly candid, I can barely stand it.

I want to cry and I don't know why.

I wanna die but instead I get high, go to the club, and hide."

I'll do anything to distract me from me

I just want to be the people that I see on TV

I'm the land of the brave and the almost free

I'm America

And I'm beautiful as can be

Sound the Alarm

Sound the alarm, something is wrong, people are tired of living a con, waking, and working, and walking away with a

payment that barely can cover their cost, plus, they're discovering flaws, look at the government totally lost,

tending to bend to the corporate agenda, depending on how they can render the laws,

open the doors, turn on the lights, see how they scatter from out of your sight, take in

the data 'cause all of it matters, and mind over matter's a matter of time,

blind, deaf, and dumb, running away from the weight of

the way that the world is confined, wrapped in a

rhythm, we're rats in a system, trapped in

religion, and money, and pride.

Uncle Larry

I haven't seen my Uncle Larry in twenty-five years. If I passed him on the street, I probably wouldn't recognize him. He hasn't maintained a relationship with me, my mom, his three children, or his grandchildren, all for various reasons that I won't go into because they aren't my stories to tell. What I will say, is the memories I have of him aren't positive.

Every summer we would visit my grandparents in Hollywood, Florida, where the humidity makes showers seem unimportant and there are more lizards than people. Uncle Larry would come by their apartment for dinners and casual socializing. He always had a scotch in hand, slowly moving the ice cubes in a circular motion, proudly showing off his gold chain, chest hair exploding out of his halfway unbuttoned shirt. He looked like Magnum, P.I., without the mustache. I don't remember much from our interactions together, but he was always promising to take me to the zoo, and never did.

I'm not sure if anyone was really certain what he did for a living, either. He was definitely an entrepreneur, but of what we were unclear. What is clear is that he was once arrested, along with nine other people, for attempting to distribute nearly forty million dollars of counterfeit traveler's checks. He was later acquitted, but we still don't know any of the details, and there were some wild family rumors floating around.

What we *do* know is that he hid a loaded gun in my grandfather's closet and didn't tell anyone about it. We know this because I found it one night.

We were visiting them for winter break and had decided to play a game where the adults hide the Chanukah presents and the kids search for them. My friend and I were on the hunt. We must have been seven or eight. I wound up at the bottom of their closet, in the den, and came across this shoebox. I opened up the lid and saw a gun lying there. Somehow in my childhood mind, I convinced myself that this was my present. I picked it up and felt the weight in my hand. Matthew was on the other side of the room. Without thinking, I pointed the gun in his direction and pulled the trigger.

"BANG!" I said, "BANG, BANG!"

Fortunately for me, and more importantly for him, the gun was on safety. I walked into the living room and asked, "Is this my present?" I remember everyone jumping up from the couch and yelling at me, "PUT THE GUN DOWN!"

The Wrong Side of History

When is it time to talk about it?

After Sandy Hook when twenty-six lives were lost
The politicians shook their heads and said
"We shouldn't talk about it."
Our nation grieved
They gave their prayers
And sent their tweets
But they didn't wanna talk about it
"We can't politicize this," they said
"Twenty kids are dead
We have to lay them to rest before we talk about it."
Like it was honoring their deaths more
To once again ignore the very reasons
But we didn't wanna talk about it
And you could take the rhetoric and switch the tragedy
I couldn't tell the difference which is obvious insanity
But I was just as culpable for what I didn't do or say

'Cause honestly it hurt too much

I didn't wanna talk about it

Well, now I wanna talk about it

Private guns have killed more Americans since 1968

Than all of our wars combined

Now personally that's a statistic that completely blows my mind

Or what about the number of our gun-related homicides?

It's higher than any other developed country by twenty times

But it's not *only* crimes, it's suicides

Every year roughly 33,000 people lose their lives

If that was terrorism we would lose our fucking minds

If that's not terrorism we have lost our fucking minds

In fact, maybe terrorism should be redefined

Because mass shootings have become a sign of modern times

Where do we draw the line?

When do we grow a spine

And stop using the second amendment to hide behind?

You wanna keep your guns, that's perfectly fine
I'm not arguing to take them away unless you're hunting lions
And yet the NRA accuses me of lying, like secretly I'm trying
That way they change the conversation from the people dying
It's really evil
I am tired of this misleading line they're feeding to the media
The talking points are really just excuses to be greedier
And Congress won't do their jobs
'Cause lobbyists have paid them off
So they ignore the problems that they're there to solve

Public service has a private interest
When campaign contributions
Make them liable to the parties that contribute
It's a form of paying tribute, but the dollars make no sense
How can a background check be something that we're against?

If the prevailing argument is,
"It's about our mental health"

Then it's illogical to think that regulations wouldn't help
And while the left and right fight, both are dying in between

It's not the red, white, and blue
It's the red, white, and green

I can't take an open water bottle on a plane
But I can walk around Nevada with an AR15

I can hear the children scream
Can't you hear the children scream?
Can't you hear the children?
Can't you hear them?
Can't you hear them scream?

You're on the wrong side of history
There is no in-between
When you look back in twenty years
Tell me who you wanna be

Can't you hear the children?
Can't you hear them?
Can't you hear them scream?

It echoes through the halls of schools
That were replaced by crime scenes

Can't you see the children?
Can't you see them?
Can't you see them bleed?
Can't you see their parents seeing them in each and every dream?

When the news vans have left

And they're left with quiet streets, and private grief

But they can't leave, they can't leave, they can't leave

So they count the seconds, minutes, hours

Days, and nights, and weeks

Dealing with a pain so deep that it's awake inside of sleep

It's in their bones, and in their smiles

And in their hair, and in their speech

And in the morning they remember

Tears streaming down their cheeks

Chest heaving from the mourning, it's impossible to breathe

And at that point it doesn't matter what you once believed

We have let a special interest hold us hostage over greed

But it's in our hands, so why are we the ones that have to . . .

FREEZE!

Don't move anything.

Don't say anything.

Don't do anything.

Don't change anything.

Dreamers

I call upon the dreamers
And the poets
And the prophets
And the seekers
Let your voices intertwine
From the stages to the speakers
From the sages to the preachers
From the artists to the teachers
There is no one that will lead us
We the people are the leaders

Together

I wish it didn't take a disaster to bring us together

I wish it didn't take a mass shooting or hurricane weather

I wish it didn't take a tragedy for us to just be better to each other
To have respect and care for one another
To look out for our sisters and our brothers
For our fathers and our mothers
No matter their religion or their colors
No matter their political opinions or the gender of their lovers
There's nothing that the human story doesn't cover

But usually we judge a book by its cover
We skip the content as if we know what we'll uncover
Then use our certainty as an excuse to blame each other

We shame each other
As if we're not the same each other

Yet when disaster strikes, we all unite

To put aside our pride and do what's *right*

We'd sacrifice our lives to do what's *right* because it's *right*

In spite of everything that came before

The very people that we used to fight, now we fight for

And it makes me wonder if that's human nature at its core

We wanna help our neighbors, we just don't know who they are

We wanna help our neighbors, we just don't know where they are

I watch him kicking down the door

Facing danger for a stranger, while I donate from afar

Wishing that I could do more

Wishing we could show the type of generosity

We do in a catastrophe

Except before

Like on the Congress floor

Shouldn't we feed the poor?

Or offer benefits for soldiers coming back from war?

Provide health care for those of us who can't afford it?

Or higher education for the next generation

Without credit card extortion?

Why can't we all agree that black lives matter?
That there aren't *fine people* that are screaming *white power*
And that *All Lives Matter* was a narcissistic trend
Where white people made *Black Lives Matter* about them

Shouldn't cops stop shooting unarmed black men?
Shouldn't women earn the same exact amount as men?

Aren't we all Americans?
Aren't we all immigrants?

Our values should be so much more important
Than our differences
Our values are what give us our significance
Our liberty was born out of ideals and innocence
An adolescent country unburdened by experience
Just naive enough to take democracy serious
Just naive enough that we could heed freedom's call
But now instead of building bridges we've resorted to a wall

Aren't we all for one?
Aren't we one for all?

Why does it have to take a tragedy for us to stand tall?
When our capacity to *give* is beyond measure

I wish it didn't take a disaster to bring us together

Empathy

It's not a human race, it's just *the* human race

There's nothing left to chase, we do not run this place

But both medicine and poison are acquired tastes

So I started taking selfies **of** somebody else's face

Forgiveness

I was raised Jewish, but I haven't practiced the traditions since right after my Bar Mitzvah. Truth be told, I've always considered myself a mediocre Jew. I don't remember any of the prayers or stories. I even fasted on the wrong holiday once.

I do identify culturally with being Jewish though, so when I was in my tattoo phase, I wanted to get a representation of my heritage. At the time, I was obsessed with the idea of forgiveness, and I thought it would be "cool" to have the Hebrew word inked on my shoulder. I went to my Rabbi, Jeff, for the translation.

After telling him what I wanted, he explained that it was against the Jewish religion to get a tattoo, but that he would make an exception for me, because he knew I would do it anyway. He photocopied the word from the prayer book. "This means forgiveness from God," he said. I went to the tattoo parlor that night.

Many years later, I was sitting on a beach in Israel with my shirt off. A guy who was from Tel Aviv, but hanging with our group, leaned over and asked me,

"Ehhhh, why do you have *Slicha* tattooed on your back?"

I turned around to face him.

"Because, as you know, it means forgiveness from God."

"Ehhhh, no it doesn't," he said.

"Ehhhh, yeah it does," I said. "My Rabbi, Jeff, told me."

"Okay, yes, maybe in the Torah," he said, "but in modern Hebrew . . . Slicha means sorry, or excuse me."

"What?"

I stared at him.

"Are you serious?"

"Yes," he said.

"So I have fucking *excuse me* tattooed on my back?"

"Yes," he said . . . "or sorry."

Security

I was going through airport security recently when a man from the TSA pulled me aside and said he needed to search through my backpack. I am usually very friendly with TSA agents. I'm aware that they are overworked, underpaid, and underappreciated, so I like to treat them with the respect they deserve.

On this particular morning, I stood by quietly as he rummaged through my property. Finally he pulled out a brown paper lunch bag filled with pita and hummus for the plane.

Now I should tell you at this point that hummus is by far my #1 snack preference. If I was stranded on an island and could only eat one thing for the rest of my life, I would choose hummus without hesitation or concern for nutritional value.

He examined the container and shook his head with authority.

"You can't bring this on the plane. It's a liquid."

"No," I replied, "it's hummus."

"No, sir, it's a liquid."

"No, sir, it's hummus. A healthy and delicious snack, made of mashed-up garbanzo beans."

"Look," he said, "I'm not gonna let you bring this through security."

I paused.

"You know this doesn't say *Hamas*, right?"

He did not find that funny.

A Piece about Peace

I have never written a piece about peace

Take the violence in the Middle East

I've watched the cycle on repeat

But who am I to comment on your grief?

When I haven't known the depths

Of your experience or your beliefs

It's simple when I say to turn the cheek

'Cause all I have to do is speak, and talk is cheap

It's painful when you've had to watch your back

While walking down the streets

Regardless of what side you're on, the history is deep

And yet we pray to different gods to get the very same relief

So at the risk of coming off like I'm trying to preach

I thought I should offer my perspective at the very least

Everywhere's a temple

Everywhere's a church

Everywhere's a mosque

Just show me where it hurts
Everywhere is sacred
So anywhere can work

Because if aliens arrive, we'll be human beings first
We are human beings first
Beyond the boundaries in the dirt
So how we treat each other
Should be how we measure our worth

And finding peace is not an external search
Forgiveness is a choice
And it's both for those who've gotten hurt
And for those who did the dirt

We're holding on to chains
And complaining that our hands are locks
Open up your palms
And watch the weight you used to carry drop
At that point, the hate will stop
Our universe is infinite and we're a tiny dot
Envision space through the perspective of an astronaut

We're chasing after God
Just be still and you'll discover he is in your heart

Every person we encounter is a work of art
You want to change the world?
Change yourself and it will start
Make a shift and everything around you takes part
Or gets taken apart

Mother Nature can be ugly
And Father Time is endless

Your enemy is a mirror if you're willing to be fearless

You could be holding the gun that's pointing at yourself
You could be dropping the bomb that's landing on your house

And I'm not saying don't protect yourself
Protect yourself
But know that revenge is against yourself

Identity is just a temporary shell
My unconscious mind perpetuates my hell
Beyond the circumstances themselves
And I don't claim to understand the circumstances themselves
But what I know is once we're here
We have to play the hands that we've been dealt

It doesn't help me blaming someone else

Or feeling sorry for myself

Or using God as an excuse to kill at will, because he's on my side

Like God would choose a side against another side

When he is every side

If we took all the energy we spent on waging war

And put it into solving our disputes instead of making more

Then maybe we could fix the problems

That we think we're fighting for

And soldiers wouldn't have to live and die in a revolving door

What are they falling for?

What are we standing for?

Let's turn the buildings that were bombed into dance floors

Our greatest pain can be our greatest celebration

But I promise it's in vain unless it brings a transformation

As above, so below

Holding space is the most important way

For giving other people room to grow

Watch what I assume to know

Take it in, but don't take it on
Or I'll respond by taking people personal
Tell my truth and let it go
By letting go of truth
I never know how someone else's truth can then affect my soul
'Cause once the conflict has started, I forget the goal
Forget the goal
I'm just a piece in a larger whole
And everything I'll ever love disintegrates to dust
So I'm the only one I'll have to learn to trust
Finding peace without war would be hard enough

It's not us versus them

It's not us versus us

It's just us

One Little Dot

How can something this big be invisible?

The environment is everywhere and yet it isn't visible
Maybe if we saw it, we would see it's not invincible
And have to take responsibility as individuals

How can something this big be invisible?

If it's all around us, it should show itself on pure principle
The scientists are certain that the damage is residual
And climate change data's reaching levels that are critical
Yet somehow that's political

We argue over math
Our citizens are too cynical to believe in facts
We make excuses and hold on to the recent past
We don't wanna sacrifice, so we refuse to ask

I grew up in a city, it's all I ever knew
So even now I have nothing to compare it to
I have to hit the park to see more than a tree or two
I have to visit nature like it's in a fucking zoo

But California was wild before the parking lots
Before the mass malls, before designer shops
Before the strip clubs, before the sea change
When mountain lions roamed freely over freeways
Before the fast food, before the freeze-frames

We live around a bunch of dead things these days

It's not an argument for better or worse

It's an observation on how we've been treating Mother Earth

See, we protect what is ours

My land

My life

My house

My kids

My job

My wife

My dog

My car

My country

My culture

But when it comes to nature our perspective is external

The planet

The forest

The ocean

The sky

The mountains

The valleys

Always *the*
never *mine*
If it's not *me*
Never mind
I'm too busy all the time
And without the ownership we ignore the warning signs

Just look at all the species on the planet that are dying
The coral reefs, the honeybees, mysteriously dying
One fourth of all the mammals that exist are dying
A third of all amphibians are at the risk of dying
We're on a path to mass extinction, it's almost like we're trying
'Cause we're relying on an atmosphere that we've been frying

I could use more statistics but you'd probably think I'm lying
Because over half the politicians we elect deny them
Well since when did their opinions outweigh the science?
I thought experiments are fundamentally unbiased

Capitalism uses nature as its example and excuse for competition
The only problem is, we've removed it from the ecosystem

Profit and balance in the market are attainable
But growth without a conscience is completely unsustainable

A lion doesn't kill *all* the gazelles

Why do we have to have it all to ourselves?

Pretty soon, there'll be nothing left but concrete and cars

And when you see an animal, it'll be like seeing a movie star

The planet

The forest

The ocean

The sky

The mountains

The valleys

Always *the*

Never *mine*

If it's not *me*

Never mind

I'm too busy all the time

And without the ownership we ignore the warning signs

Our planet

Our forest

Our ocean

Our sky

Our mountains

Our valleys
Always *we*
Always *mine*

My planet
My forest
My ocean
My sky
My mountains
My valleys
Always *we*
Always *mine*
Always *ours*
Always *yours*

One little dot in trillions of stars

One little dot, it's all that we've got

We just forgot that none of it's ours

We just forgot that all of it's ours

One little dot in trillions of stars

Mirrors

We are all mirrors
Codesigners of this human experience
So this is not my voice that you're hearing
It is ours
I'm here as a reflection
To remind you of your inner power
In my next life, I'll be a sunflower

See, we belong to the world
It's not the other way around
So I vow to keep my head inside the clouds
And my feet on solid ground
The stimulus is infinite, in and out
It's common to forget what life is all about

What is life all about?
If all that counts is the numbers in our bank accounts
Happiness cannot be found by having an amount
It's what we do that counts

It's who we are to the people that we care about
It's who we are to the people we don't care about
Because anyone could be someone we could care about

What if humanity had grown up in your parents' house?

What if everyone you see is family?

Think about how much you love the people that you love
And love all people with the same capacity

Compassion is an action
And actually, so is atrophy
It takes as much effort to create
As it takes to pass our time passively

Yesterday's the future
Tomorrow is the past
This moment is an instant
It's over in a flash

Our bodies turn to ash
Recycled by the dirt

The only thing that really lasts is the energy on earth

Because when we breathe out, the plants breathe in
Then the plants breathe out, and the cycle starts again

We're in a human chess match against our evolution
We used to focus on our problems, now we're open to solutions
Technology could be the catalyst for revolution
Community is as important as an institution
These lines are an illusion

We could be anywhere, and anywhere would still be here

Do you hear? Are you here?
The people aren't over there
Over where?
There is only here
Have I made my message clear?

I see myself through my words
Like I wrote this on a mirror

What we are doing now is the next hundred years
What we are doing now is the next thousand years

I dare you to be beautiful, but first be aware

However you perceive is the way that you appear

High Tide

The universe doesn't respond to a lie
No matter how hard you try, the truth will not be denied

It doesn't judge and it doesn't choose sides
It just attaches to the frequency and matches the vibe

The universe doesn't respond to a lie
It's the space in between where the stars live and die

There's a black hole sitting in the iris of my eye
So it sucks the world in and then gets lost in my mind

The universe doesn't respond to a lie
It connects, then reflects, to the deeper truth inside

I'm a sandcastle

But I fell in love with high tide

And if she takes me away

It's all a part of the ride

Keep Loving: Part III

Keep loving through your shadow

Keep loving through your light

Keep loving through your mornings

Keep loving through your nights

Keep loving through your losses

Keep loving through your wins

Keep loving through beginnings

Keep loving through the ends

Keep loving through your yes's

Keep loving through your no's

Keep loving through your blessings

Keep loving through your growth

Keep loving through your movement

Keep loving through your breath

Keep loving until loving is the only thing that's left

I Am

You don't have to be loved, to be love

You are love

You don't have to be, you just have to be

Can you see?

You don't have to be loved, to be love

You are love

It's what you're made of

There's nothing to become

It's what you came from

Love

It emanates from everything you do

There is no one to compare yourself to

There is only love

Even when it's hate

It's still love

You just have to wait long enough
Eventually it's showing up
I think it's showing off
Look at all the disguises it's pulling off
But underneath it all

Love

The building blocks of civilization
The mantra that anchors me in my meditations
The frequency that activates a manifestation
The source of all creation
There is no limitation

Love

The more you give, the more you gain
Because you can't lose what you contain
It's an equation that I can't explain
You'd have to think outside your brain
You'd have to let the pain pass through you like a mighty rain
You'd have to celebrate your hate, without resorting to blame
Only then can circumstances change
You know the name of it

Love

They'll tell you that it comes from up above
But it comes from deep inside
When there's nowhere left to hide
When you take responsibility for being on this ride
When you refuse to dramatize or victimize, you can rise
When you judge without your judgments
And you're proud without your pride
That's the moment you'll feel most alive

I can't deny
I'm still attached to being unattached
I'm holding on to letting go

But I will not achieve my goals until I can receive my goals
'Cause I will not express my soul unless I do not need your love
I must accept myself without exception, then I'll be your love

I wish that I was good enough to make **you** see *your* love

But being good enough will never let me lead from love

I'd have to bleed from love

I'd have to grieve from love

I'd have to breathe from love

Can you see *my love?*

Acknowledgments

I'd like to start off by thanking the very woman who didn't hear it enough from me growing up. To my beautiful mother, Ellen Schmalholz. Your acknowledgments should be their own book. You deserved a thank-you from me every day of my life. I owe you everything, Mom. You single-handedly raised me into the man I am today. Thank you for your love, your sacrifice, your strength, and your unending support. You are my hero.

To my partner and best friend, Andriana Manfredi. Thank you for showing me what unconditional love *truly* is. Thank you for loving me through my anger, my joy, my sadness, my fears, my failures, and my successes. You have made everything in my life infinitely better.

To my manager and brother, Kevin Hekmat. Words don't do justice. I would not be here without you. You created the vision for my career and allowed me the freedom to focus on my writing and performing. Thank you for having my back in every possible situation. Thank you for your honesty, your optimism, your patience, your humor, your intellect, and your integrity. I deeply respect and admire how you show up in the world.

To my friend and colleague, Gali Firstenberg. Thank you for bringing your love, your talent, your passion, and your dedication to everything we've built as a team. You helped elevate us to the next level in every way.

To my literary agent, Andrea Barzvi. Thank you for believing in my poetry and making this project possible in the first place. We would not be here without you. Your vision, wisdom, and experience have been invaluable in turning this idea into a reality. I am beyond grateful.

To my editors, Gideon Weil and Sydney Rogers. Thank you for gracefully leading me through the creative process and communicating with such clarity. Your expertise, perspective, and guidance helped me to tell a deeper and more authentic story. I'd also like to acknowledge Judith Curr and the entire team at HarperOne and HarperCollins Publishers for bringing this book to life. You have *all* given a home to my art.

To Mustashrik Mahbub. Thank you for interpreting my words into such beautiful and thoughtful illustrations. Your images bring a new meaning and depth into my poetry. I am so proud of what we created together. You are a true artist.

To A&E, Life Is Beautiful, Life Is Good, Stephen, and ZHU. Thank you for collaborating on poems that were included in the book. I couldn't ask for better partners.

To my lawyer and friend, Ken Hertz, Jon Polk, and everyone at Hertz Lichtenstein & Young, LLP. Thank you for always protecting my interests and supporting my career.

To everyone who read the earlier stages of the manuscript. Thank you for helping me to shape the narrative of the poems and stories. It was an honor to get your feedback and I was truly moved by how people showed up for me during this process. I'd like to specifically highlight Alex Banayan and Shihan Van Clief for going above and beyond with their time and energy. You all pushed me to reach my fullest potential.

To Da Poetry Lounge community. Thank you for being like a second family to me and the foundation for my poetry career. Some of the most incredible art experiences I've ever had were as an audience member at The Greenway Court Theatre. Dante Basco, Shihan, Poetri, Gimel Hooper, Omari Hardwick, Azikiwe Andrews, GaKnew Roxwel, Gina Loring, Javon Johnson, Joe Hernandez-Kolski, Joshua Silverstein, Justine Bae, Natalie Patterson, Oveous, Rudy Francisco, Sekou Andrews, Steve Connell, Thea Monyee, Tshaka Campbell, Yesika Salgado, and the countless other poets who have inspired me to create. I honor you.

To my mentor and brother, Ross Hogarth. There is no way I could acknowledge you enough. You gave me your advice, time, talent, generosity, and love when I needed them most. You created opportunities for me and shared your wisdom selflessly. I am a better person and artist because of our friendship. I thank you from the bottom of my heart.

To Tim James, Antonina Armato, and Rock Mafia studios. I am forever grateful. It's been over a decade of creating music together and we have become like a family. Thank you for taking a chance on signing me when no one else would. You opened up your doors and gave me the creative space to explore my songwriting and pursue my poetry. Thomas Sturges, Sam Sturges, Adam Comstock, Steve Hammons, DK, Jon Vella, Danny Parra, and the many producers, writers, engineers, and artists who put their hearts and souls into their music. I appreciate you.

To my Amigos: Alex Banayan, Austin Bisnow, Elliott Bisnow, and Mike Posner. Each of you inspire me to be a better version of myself. It's rare to make such an amazing group of close friends at this stage in life. I feel lucky that I get to call you my brothers.

To Rachel Putter, Robert Resnick, and Sylvie Targhetta. I cannot imagine where I would be without your many insights. Thank you for being a light in the dark. I will try to pay it forward.

A special thanks goes out to the following communities: Cirque du Soleil, Conscious Capitalism, Daybreaker, Def Poetry Jam, FlyPoet, Inner Light Media, Landmarks Live, Magic Giant, Modo Yoga LA, One Drop Foundation, (RED), School of Greatness, Sideshow Collectibles, SuperSoul 100, The Actor's Lounge, The Greenway Court Theatre, Verses & Flow, WORLDZ, and Ziva Meditation. I am honored to be included in your tribes.

Specifically, I'd like to acknowledge the Summit community for its impact and influence on me. Some of my best memories and relationships were made on the mountain. Thank you, Elliott

Bisnow, Jeff Rosenthal, Brett Leve, Jeremy Schwartz, and the en-
tire Summit Series team, for expanding my circle of friendship and
vision of what is possible.

I'd also like to acknowledge PTTOW! for opening doors to new
partnerships and creative opportunities. You gave me a platform
to impact larger audiences through my poetry. Thank you, Roman
Tsunder, Terry Hardy, James Sullos, and the rest of the PTTOW!
team, for welcoming us into your community.

And finally to my closest friends, family, and creative collabora-
tors, you have *all* profoundly influenced my life and art: Jeremiah
Santos, Joshua Temkin, Justin Doff, Adam Ward, Alex Wagmiester,
Alexandra Spitz, Allie Michelle, Aloe Blacc, Andre Herd, Atticus,
Aubrey Marcus, Barbara Bozman, Barbara Temkin, Ben Gleib,
Ben Nemtin, Bert & John Jacobs, Braelinn Frank, Brenda Reynoso,
Cal Fussman, Chrysi Philalithes, Clark Langon, Craig Clemens,
Dakota Adan, Daniel Catullo, Daniel N. Johnson, Darren Wilson,
David Helfant, David Kabiller, Devin Powers, Dhru Purohit, Diana
Gouveia, Eli Clark-Davis, Emily Fletcher, Emily Greener, Emily
Morwen, Ethan Lipsitz, Gayle Troberman & Sue Turner, Grace
Bowden, Greg Anzalone, Hiba Abu-Baker, Ida Darvish, Jacklyn
Uweh, Jake Udell, Jay Faires, John Manulis, Johnny Pfieger, Joshua

Bozman, Josiah Stein, Joy Rheman, Julia & River Rosenthal, Julie Hovsepian, Julie Pilat, Justin Dangel, Justin Weniger, Kevin Bailey, Kevin Vilkin, Kris & Brady Hogarth, Leonard Armato, Lewis Howes, Liz Heller, Louie Schwartzberg, Mark & Margot Bisnow, Mark Foster, Morgan McGrath, Murray Hidary, Najwa Zebian, Nic Rolston, Nicole Davis & Lumi, Noa Tishby & Ari, Pierson Blaetz, Quddus Philippe, Rabbi Jeff, Radha & Miki Agrawal, Ramy Youssef, Rich Roll & Julie Piatt, Ross Hinkle, Ryland Engelhart, Sonya Samuels, Sophia Bentaher, Steven Vincent, Susan Schacher, Teri Hertz, Travis Be, Tyler Wakstein, Unjoo Moon & Dion Beebe, The Ames family, The Browns, David Scott & family, Deena, JJ, & the Robertson family, The Hardwicks, The Hoopers, Jay Schmalholz & family, Kamyar, Shilla, Paulina & the Hekmat family, The Levin family, The Messingers, The Moores, Paige Little-Ward & family, The Parrents, The Smiths, The Swartz family, The Van Cliefs, The Weiss family. I love you all.

This book is in loving memory of Dotty & Al Schmalholz, Casey Shearer, Dolores Freedman, Sean Stephenson, and Marley.

Index of Poems

Inhale

Exhale

Index by Theme

Love

Family

Inspiration & Lessons

Stories

Collaborations

Look Closer in partnership with A+E Networks

Dreamers in partnership with Life Is Beautiful Festival

Superpowers in partnership with *Life Is Good: The Book*

The New You in partnership with Stephen Swartz
for the song "Start a Fire"

Higher View and Empathy in partnership with ZHU
for the song "Good Life"

About the Author

IN-Q is a National Poetry Slam champion, award-winning poet, and multiplatinum songwriter. His groundbreaking achievements include being named to Oprah's SuperSoul 100 list of the world's most influential thought leaders, being the first spoken-word artist to perform with Cirque du Soleil, and being featured on A&E, ESPN, and HBO's *Def Poetry Jam*. He's inspired audiences around the world through his live performances and storytelling workshops. Many of his recent poetry videos have gone viral, with over 70 million views combined.

As a songwriter, IN-Q's hit single "Love You Like a Love Song" by Selena Gomez went multiplatinum, winning him a BMI award. He has written with renowned artists including Aloe Blacc, Miley Cyrus, Mike Posner, and Foster the People. His songs have accumulated over one billion views on YouTube alone.

Leading organizations including Nike, Instagram, Spotify, Google, Lululemon, Live Nation, Shazam, The GRAMMY Foundation, and many more have brought IN-Q in to motivate their teams through his keynote speeches and acclaimed storytelling workshops.

Ultimately IN-Q writes to entertain, inspire, and challenge his audiences to look deeper into the human experience and ask questions about themselves, their environment, and the world at large.